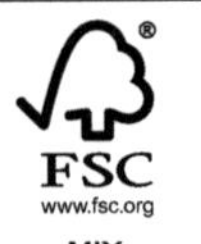

Andreas Weiland

The Blackness of
Black

In Memory of
Nan Hoover

STONYBROOK EDITIONS

Andreas Weiland, The Blackness of
Black.Poems in Memory of Nan Noover.
© Stonybook Editions, 2022

Herstellung und Verlag:
BoD – Books on Demand, Norderstedt
ISBN: 9783756247578

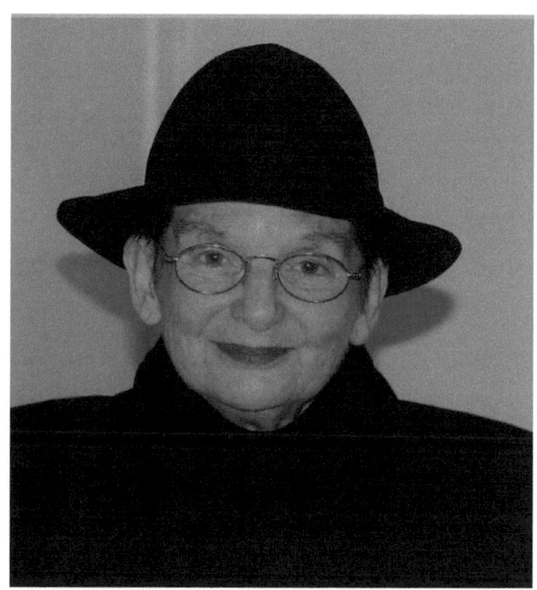

Nan Hoover, *by Myriam Thyes*

BLACK IS NORTH

1

Black is NORTH
long winter nights
the dark clouds driven
by the Siberian wind
Black is the eye's center
A shiny pupil, recording
the throb of life

Blown past,
in the night wind
black is the reflection
of the great,
unknown ideogram

Black flows apart, to the
ends of the world
and then, back again
at the end of night
it is extending
from light to light

2

within blackness
the light is
            swallowed
stored, piled up
layer upon layer
            upon layer

THE SLANTED MOON

1

the slanted moon
cushioned in fogs of light
half-blackened
        by shadow

stood on the night's sky
out there
in that dark tunnel
of a space filled by pulsating forces

2

the moon is a face in the night
is – frightened eyes
dark, in the shadow
Is a left cheek,
        now dark now light
Is a right one,
        glistening
with brightness

3

the ghostlike mask
of a face
suddenly appears
in the light of a lantern

the dark outline of a body
sinks again
into the shadow
of things

THE WOMAN

1

the woman
(her face
        lighted up
in the darkness)
looks into night
with deep, black eyes

2

in the quietness of the world
all light comes from within
Saw it stream
        from her
through her
        translucent skin

3

the dynamo of her life
disperses light
over her cheek-bone

and onto her
hands, even

HEAD IN THE CLOUDS

1

head in the clouds...
rhomb-shaped
patterns of light
puzzling the eye

that is tracing the secrets
of the firmament
as he walks on
on the terrestrial disk

2

the plant-shaped man
has curly leaves
extending into legs

ribs bared
in front of the empty ocean
of the sky...

3

the sea clouds flood
the ancient ground behind
a mirrored, inverse universe
of life

where she confronts him
blood stained, quiet cunt
in no man's lands of light...

4

faces turned to the sun
an upper-world of make-believe of words

split-second reasons
hunted down by wolves

her hands
reach out of darkness
into now...

WARM, FERTILE CAVE

1

warm, fertile cave
pregnant with darkness
Saw
earthen pottery
under the
bread-fruit tree
of a land
once known

2

from which were driven
delights
from which were driven –
none of the desires
"Where do you go? Eve you
dark mother"

3

from out of the deep
a cry is rushing
it is the inaudible sound
of light

4

I see houses,
standing slanted
            in the wind
I feel the wind that is
keeping them
            from falling

5

    leaves, light-sick
blow away
        in the heat of noon
basked, singed
        sunk
                in dust

6

and as white
    as flour

7

walking, I felt
  the grasses piercing
the bloodied flesh

                felt,
          the tipped-over
                    amphora

          light-flooded –
              embroidered
                    by shadow

THE CURTAIN OF REALITY

1

the curtain of reality
the vast cloud
of which only

some tiny particle
(the giant eye of GOD)
appears in front of our eyes, gets
into the eye, the eyes

Can't be wiped off, you understand
All those cascades of rain
while the cloud
OPENS,

white and
wind-beaten,
the hachure
of storm
in the face
of the hidden sky

2

torn open, suddenly
  the crack, in the
            rain curtain:
Lightning flashes
            in the dark

3

What lies behind it?
Those deep
            eye sockets…
Worlds deep &
      graduated –
Box within
            box
         within box?

4

white curtain
         black curtain
one slides
         in front of
            the other

SOAKED, BY CASCADES OF RAIN

1

soaked by cascades of rain
enlightened by flashing lightning
passed the black promontory
of night

2

the sea is a vast nothingness
where moonlight drew
its silvery trace

3

our shadows step forward
in iridescent floods
the lighted road ends

REMEMBERING NAN HOOVER

"it is not so important how we look at something but rather how we perceive this can be done in a second and last decades or a life time"
Nan Hoover in 'night letters'

The American artist Nan Hoover was born in New York City, on May 12, 1931, during the Great Depression. Between 1948 and 1952, she studied at the Concoran School of the Arts and Design in Washington, D.C. Her early work consisted mostly of paintings. It was still influenced by surrealism at the beginning.

Since the early 1970s, Nan Hoover has lived mostly in the Netherlands.[1] She also lived in Düsseldorf, Germany, for some time. She died in Berlin in 2008.

Today, Nan Hoover is well-known as a pioneer of minimalist video art and, together with Marina Abramović, and Tony Morgan, as a noteworthy live performer who gained attention both in New York, in Düsseldorf and in Amsterdam.

In fact, this happened especially in Amsterdam, where the gallery De Appel, at its old and almost forgotten Brouwersgracht address, was the decisive location where these artists who were not yet widely known by the time, could reach out to an attentive public. And this largely thanks to the unforgettable Wies Smals (born 1939) who would unfortunately die in 1983 in a plane accident when she was, at age 44, still so young.[2]

I first met Nan Hoover in Essen in the 1980s, at a time when she lived in Düsseldorf, a center of artists connected in one way or other with the Fluxus movement. She had been in contact already with such Düsseldorf-based artists as Daniel Spoerri (b. 1930), Robert Filliou (1926-1987), and Tony Morgan (1938-2004) before. And now she got in touch with others like Werner Nekes (1944-2017), with Werner's wife Dore O. (1946-2022) and with Doris Schoettler-Boll (1945-2015) who invited her to the noted exhibition "Unter einem Himmel" (in English: Under One and The Same Sky (Essen, 1987-'88).[3]

Nan Hoover's work, at the time, already consisted largely of experimental video films, performances and light installations. She was still a fine painter, a creator of delicate drawings, a photographer and sculptor.

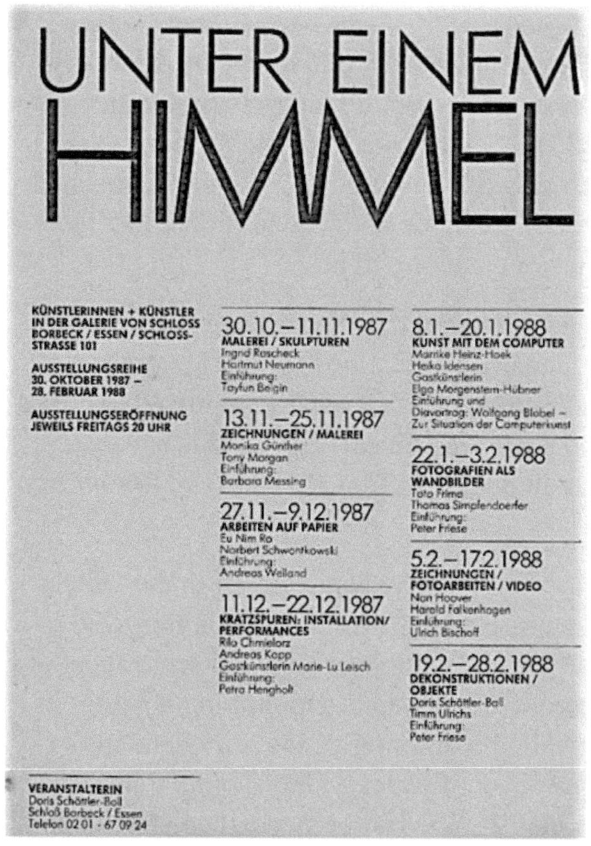

Critics have repeatedly noted that since the 1970s, Nan Hoover's art has been focused on "light and motion." Indeed, an unnamed critic is describing light and motion as "her theme." I do not quite agree. Based on how I saw her work as a video artist, I would not speak of a theme but of a very conscious exploration of material possibilities, coupled with an extremely sensitive, largely intuitive way of handling things. This approach often reveals a subtle, delicate motion under the influence of changing light.

Like others interested in Nan Hoover's art, the quoted unnamed critic does not fail to notice a certain "minimalism" of means employed to create rich and surprising visual effects. This is very apparent in her video film *Returning to Mount Fuji* (1984).

When I was invited by Nan Hoover in the 1980s, she let me see how she produced this film with minimal means, holding a white A4 sized sheet of paper in one of her hands and moving it gently in the air while photographing these movements of the white sheet of paper with her small video camera that she let change its position slowly and perhaps quite intuitively.

While she was doing this, the warm sunlight of a summer day fell through a nearby window of her apartment onto the sheet of paper that was continuously changing, very minimally, its angle, moving up or down as well as sideways, gently like a boat on slightly stirred waves. The light shed onto the white paper created a surprising richness of warm whites, sometimes approaching a crème-colored variety of tones.

In the finished movie, such an approach that was very conscious of the scope of formal possibilities inscribed in the use of a minimal number of material inputs (the sheet of paper, the sunlight, the human hand that would not be visible in the video film, and the camera), evokes a meditative atmosphere. At the same time, it can let us see imaginary landscapes, like Mount Fuji, in changing light. All of this confirms the observation of yet another unnamed critic that her works tend to be "both formalist and highly sensual" and that her "meticulous renderings of light, color and movement" can "suggest external and interior landscapes."

Indeed, what Nan Hoover was demonstrating in Düsseldorf during my visit was a way of "fluidly manipulating light and shadow into sculptural form" – or, in fact, in the Mt. Fuji video film, not really into a sculptural form, in the singular, but into the changing forms of an imaginary, virtually three-dimensional object: a mountain. In this way, the assessment that she could create "an evocative tension between abstraction and reality" (the created visual image and the real landscape, the mountain referred to, by way of the film's title) is shown as correct.[4]

I agree that video art works like *Returning to Mt. Fuji* and that her live performances reveal, again and again, her "minimalist handling of her means as well as the intense concentration with which she performed within spaces of light and shadow." And it makes sense to affirm that this kind "handling" and this intensity of concentration "are the most salient characteristics" of her artistic approach.

Most certainly, this is true of the specific video I have mentioned, and more generally, of a performance artist who has given us, in the last three decades of the 20th century, inspiring examples of an idealistic, sometimes mediative, always imagination-based, and yet materially explorative rapprochement to the visible realities of our world that mattered most to her.

Nan Hoover's innovative artistic achievement has been recognized by invitations to take part in the internationally renowned documenta (in 1977, and again, later) and in the Biennale di Venezia (in 1984).

In 1986, Nan Hoover taught briefly at the San Francisco Art Institute, but then opted to stay in Europe as an expatriate American artist because she may have felt that it was here where her work was most clearly appreciated, even though only by a minority. A few years before her death in 2008, she moved to Berlin.

- Andreas Weiland

Notes

[1] After having stayed in Paris and London, according to one source, she settled down in Amsterdam in 1969.

[2] I first met Wies Smals a short time before my departure to Taiwan in 1976 where I taught 20th century German literature for a couple of years. This encounter occurred during the performance of Tony Morgan's live performance entitled very aptly, just like his video film, "Herman Dances Alone" (for which I had written the catalogue text; the film title can also be deciphered as "her man dances alone"). I later corresponded with Wies and the poet Martha Hawley (who was also closely collected with the gallery) while in Taiwan, at a time when I was writing articles for ARTIST MAGAZINE (Yishu jia), for YINXIANG (MAGAZINE) and STREET, and attempted to organize an exhibition of Robert Filliou's work in a renowned Taipei gallery. Unsuccessfully, I admit, because the problem of who would pay for transport and insurance of Filliou's work could not be resolved. The recent website of the new DE APPEL gallery still mentions Wies Smals and it

also names Marina Abramović's partner Ulay. Both lived together, in a high-rise building in *Noord*-Amsterdam. Marina invited Tony and me one day; Tony and she had a lot to talk about; I still remember how skeptical I was with regard to her 20th century, post-modern "mysticism"… The De Appel website also mentions such artists as Ben d'Armagnac, Gerrit Dekker, Bruce Nauman, James Lee Byars and Joan Jonas, but is silent about Nan Hoover.

[3] This was, in a way, a feminist exhibition, to the extent that in each of the shows of this long series of expos featuring always two artists in that summer, the curating artist, Doris Schoettler-Boll, always paired one female and one male artist, in order to let the audience sense the similarities and differences of works that focused on the same theme. Nan Hoover chose Harald Falkenhagen as the artist who would, just like she, focus on "blackness." The title of the expo, "Below one and the same sky" in English, is a title that alluded to the saying 妇女能顶半边天 - "women hold up half the sky" / Frauen sind die Hälfte des Himmels.

[4] "Nan Hoover's works are both formalist and highly sensual. Her meticulous renderings of light, color and movement suggest external and interior landscapes. Fluidly manipulating light and shadow into sculptural form, Hoover creates an evocative tension between abstraction and reality."
(http://www.imagine-space.net/pages/namen/hoover.html)

**Performances and Light Installations of
Nan Hoover**

1974 Kudamm Performance, at Kurfürstendamm,
Berlin, Germany

1975 (without title), American Hotel, Amsterdam,
Nederland (i.e. The Netherlands=NL)

1976 Silence, Studiogalerie, Berlin, Germany

1976 Light Shapes, De Appel, Amsterdam, NL

1977 Light Composition, Martinkerk,
Zomermanifestatie, NL

1977 Body in Landscape, Kunstverein Frankfurt,
Germany

1978 On the Edge of Light, Filkingen, Stockholm,
Sweden

1978 Movement in Dark, Galerie Waalkens,
Finsterwolde, NL

1978 Light News, Anna Canepa, New York, US,
with Sam Schoenbaum

1978 High Performance, Los Angeles, US

1978 Véhicule, Montreal, Canada

1979 Progressions, Video im Abendland,
Kölnischer Kunstverein, Cologne, Germany

1981 Doors, Neuer Berliner Kunstverein, Berlin,
Germany

1981 Through Dark Shadows, Heidelberger
Kunstverein, Heidelberg, Germany

1982 Intercept the Rays, Kunstzaal Markt 17,
Enschede, NL

1985 Walking in Any Direction, Long Beach
Museum of Art, US

1985 Extensions of Light, San Francisco Art
Institute, US

1987 Light Composition, Documenta 8, Kassel,
Germany

1993 Light for Richard, Zoetermeer, NL

1995 Movement in Light, Performance Festival,
Kunstakademie Düsseldorf, Germany

1995 movement from either direction, Kunst- und
Ausstellungshalle der Bundesrepublik
Deutschland, Bonn, Germany

2008 Desert, during the National Review of Live
Arts at the Tramway, Glasgow, UK

2008 Some Times with Bill Viola, Salzburg
Museum der Moderne, Austria

Exhibitions of Nan Hoover

1975 Galerie Jurka, Amsterdam, Nederland / The Netherlands (video, photographs - cat.)

1976 De Appel, Amsterdam, The Netherlands (video installation, video, film)

1976 Studiogalerie, Berlin, Germany (photographs, video, performance)

1977 London Film Co-op, London, UK (video)

1977 Museum of Modern Art, New York, USA (video)

1978 Anthology Film Archives, New York, USA (video)

1979 Art Metropole, Toronto, Canada (video)

1979 Stedelijk Museum, Amsterdam (photo installation, photographs, video)

1980 Museum of Modern Art, New York, USA (video installation)

1980 Museum Fodor, Amsterdam (photographs)

1981 Biederberg/Wetering Galerie, Amsterdam
(light objects, light installations)

1981 The Bank, Amsterdam, The Netherlands
(video)

1981 Stedelijk Museum, Schiedam, The
Netherlands (photographs, video, cat.)

1981 Künstlerhaus Stuttgart, Germany
(photographs, video - cat.)

1981 Neue Galerie, Aachen, Germany
(photographs - cat.)

1981 DAAD Gallery, Berlin, Germany
(photographs, video - cat.)

1982 Long Beach Museum of Art, California,
USA (video)

1982 Musée d'Art Contemporain, Montréal
(photographs, video, performance - cat.)

1983 A.I.R. London Video Arts, London, UK
(video)

1983 Montevideo, Amsterdam, The Netherlands
(video)

1984 Het Kijkhuis, The Hague, The Netherlands
(video)

1984 Video Kooperative, Cologne, Germany
(video)

1984 Montevideo, Amsterdam, The Netherlands
(video)

1984 Molkerei Werkstatt, Cologne, Germany
(light installation)

1984 Time Based Arts, Amsterdam, The
Netherlands (video installation)

1984 Het Kijkhuis, The Hague, The Netherlands
(photographs, video)

1985 Arsenal, Berlin, Germany (film)

1985 Anthology Film Archives, New York (video)

1985 San Francisco Cinematheque, California,
USA (video)

1985 De Vleeshal, Middelburg, with Marijk van
Dyck (light installation - cat.)

1985 Galerie Paladijn, Amsterdam (photo objects,
photographs, video)

1986 Kettle's Yard, Cambridge, UK (photographs, objects, video - cat.)

1986 Matt's Gallery, London, UK (photographs, objects, video - cat.)

1987 Galerie René Coëlho, Amsterdam, The Netherlands (photographs, video)

1987 Het Kijkhuis, The Hague, The Netherlands (video installations)

1988 Museum für Gegenwartskunst, Basel, Switzerland (video, film)

1988 Kunsthaus Zürich, Switzerland (video)

1988 Kunstmuseum Bern, Switzerland (video, film)

1988 "Licht met papier - fotografie en video", Gemeentehuis Bloemendaal, Overveen, The Netherlands

1988 "Unter einem Himmel", Schloss Borbeck, Essen, with Harald Falkenhagen (paintings; drawings), curated by Doris Schöttler-Boll

1988 Kunstmuseum Bern. (drawings - cat.)

1988 "Photoszene Köln 1988", Nada Art, Cologne, Germany

1989 Museum Folkwang, Essen, Germany (drawings, video - cat.)

1989 Galerie Piwna, Warsaw, Poland (drawings)

1989 Galerie Potocka, Cracow, Poland (drawings - cat.)

1990 Galerie Katrin Rabus, Bremen, Germany, with Harald Falkenhagen (drawings)

1990 Galerie Pennings, Eindhoven, The Netherlands (photographs)

1991 The Kitchen, New York, USA (video retrospective)

1991 Neue Pinakothek, Munich, Germany, parallel to John Cage (drawings, video)

1991 Galerie René Coëlho, Amsterdam, The Netherlands (video retrospective, photocollage of performances 1974-1988)

1991 Suzanne Biederberg Galerie, Amsterdam, The Netherlands (drawings, sculptures)

1991 Stedelijk Museum, Amsterdam, The
Netherlands (drawings)

1991 "Thrusting Forms", Island Mountain Gallery,
Wells, B.C., Canada (drawings, video)

1991 Delta Galerie, Düsseldorf, Germany (video,
photographs, drawings)

1992 "Out/In Fuhrwerkswaage" light installation
in Kunstraum Fuhrwerkswaage, Cologne,
Germany in the framework of "Kunst Licht
Konzepte Raum", curated by Christian Merscheid

1992 Galerie Am Luxemburgplatz, Wiesbaden,
Germany (drawings, photographs, video)

1993 "innerer Raum" (inner space), Institut für
künstlerische Forschung, Düsseldorf, Germany
(light installation)

1994 "Malkasten", Düsseldorf, Germany (with
Birgitta Thaysen) (paintings, drawings,
installation, wood relief)

1994 Galerie Fotohof, Salzburg, Austria
(photography and video installation)

1994 Artothek Köln, Cologne, Germany (drawings

and installations)

1995 Museum Wiesbaden, Wiesbaden, Germany (video installation)

1995 Galerie Patrik Fröhlich, Bern, Switzerland (sculpture, drawings and photographs)

1995 Galerie Ulrike Buschlinger, Wiesbaden, Germany (drawings, wood reliefs, video installation)

1995 Kunst- und Ausstellungshalle der Bundesrepublik Deutschland, Bonn, "movement from either direction" (video installation)

1996 Kunstverein Heilbronn, Heilbronn, Germany (drawings, video installations and wood reliefs)

1996 Art Cologne, Ulrike Buschlinger Galerie, Wiesbaden, Germany (drawings, video installation, photographs)

1997 Galerie grada Zagreba, Zagreb, Croatia (drawings, photographs, video installation)

1997 Galerie Patrik Fröhlich, Zürich, Switzerland (drawings, photographs, video installation)

1997 Museum Wiesbaden, Wiesbaden, Germany
(light installation, performance)

1997 's-Heerenberg, The Netherlands (light
installation, performance)

1997 "Project of Art in Castles", Euregio: Drittes
Niederrheinisches Herrensitzspektakel, Kasteel
Bergh

1997 Galerie im Winter, Bremen, Germany
(photographs, drawings, video tapes)

1997 Galerie Hubertus Wunschik, Düsseldorf,
Germany (photographs, drawings, video
installation, video tapes)

1998 Galerija sodobne umetnosti Celje, Celje,
Slovenia (drawings, photographs, 2 video
installations, video tapes)

1998 Les Jardins d'hiver, Emporio Armani,
Brussels, Belgium (photographs, photo object)

1998 Aschenbach Galerie, Amsterdam, The
Netherlands (drawings, photographs, video object)

1998 Galerie Ulrike Buschlinger, Wiesbaden,
Germany (drawings, photographs, video object)

1998 Salon, San Miguel de Allende, Mexico
(photographs, video)

1998 Albrecht Dürer Gesellschaft, Nürnberg,
Germany (drawings, photographs, video tapes)

1999 Galerie Patrik Fröhlich, Zürich, Switzerland
(photographs, drawings)

1999 'Kunst 99' Art Fair Zurich,
Galerie Patrik Fröhlich, Switzerland (photographs,
drawings)

2000 ART COLOGNE - Galerie Ulrike
Buschlinger, Wiesbaden, Germany (photographs,
video installations)

2000 Galerie Doris Wullkopf, Lindau-Insel,
Germany

2001 Staatliche Galerie Moritzburg, Halle,
Germany

2001 Nederlands Instituut voor Mediakunst -
Montevideo / Time Based Arts, Amsterdam, NL:
DIALOGUE - works by Nan Hoover, August /
September

2002 Galerie Dany Keller, Munich, Germany, July

/ August: black and white - interactive video installation

2002 Galerie Patrik Fröhlich, Zürich, Switzerland, September

2002 Galerie Ernst Hilger, Wien, Austria, December

2003 Galerie Ulrike Buschlinger, Wiesbaden, Germany, Jan. / Feb.

2003 Kunsthalle Darmstadt: 'some times'- Nan Hoover: photography, Bill Viola: video projections. June 2 - Aug. 3.

2003 ominous mountains 1, Galerie Hubertus Wunschik, Mönchengladbach, Germany, 'ominous mountains' by Nan Hoover. June 6 - Aug. 2.

2003 Oct. 8 - 25, Suzanne Biederberg Gallery, Amsterdam, Netherlands.

2003 Amsterdam / Echigo Tsumari - Nan Hoover

2004 Sebastian Fath Contemporary, Mannheim, Germany: Nan Hoover - photo works.March 4 till April 11. - Flying Feet, Nan Hoover 1978

2005 Metis Gallery, Amsterdam, Netherlands: Nan Hoover, photography and two video sculptures, 10 September till 8 October.

2006 Galerie Ulrike Buschlinger, Wiesbaden, Germany. Photography.

2006 Museum Wiesbaden, Germany. Three Installations, with catalogue.

2006 Sebastian Fath Contemporary, Mannheim, Germany: "Landschaft", drawings, paintings, sculptures, video.

2007 Dieter Reitz Gallery, Berlin, Germany. Drawings / video / light installation, August 3 - September 22, 2007.

2007 Gallery Reitz: works from the exhibition: photographs | pastel drawings

2007 dsART Gallery Frankfurt/Main, Germany, September.

2008 MdM Mönchsberg, Museum der Moderne, Salzburg, Austria: Nan Hoover / Bill Viola. Some Times - video, photography, March - July

2008 Sebastian Fath Contemporary, Mannheim,

Germany: Nan Hoover - Photography and
Drawings, June – July

2008 Dieter Reitz Gallery, Berlin. Nan Hoover -
Hands, Sep. 25 – Nov. 8

2008 Suzanne Biederberg Gallery, Amsterdam,
The Netherlands: Nan Hoover: Gestures - Closing
Doors, Nov. - Dec.

See also:
https://www.nanhooverfoundation.com/artworks.html

Magdi Youssef

A FEW WORDS ABOUT THE POET AND ART CRITIC ANDREAS WEILAND

The author of the poems in this small volume, Andreas Weiland, published his first poems in The Q, a literary journal edited by the novelist and poet John Sawkins, M.A. and others – all of them based at the English Dept. at RUB Ruhr University in Bochum. This was in 1967, and in the same year, his poems (in English) appeared in a literary and film journal, Touch, published in Philadelphia, PA and Bochum by Weiland and Steven R. Diamant, a poet, archeologist, and friend of Robert Kelly and Guy Davenport.

In 1968, Michael Horovitz, the noted celebrity of English "underground poetry" and editor of the poetry anthology The Children of Albion: Poetry of the Underground in Britain, came to Bochum for a joint poetry reading with Weiland. In that year, Weiland also visited Robert Filliou in Düsseldorf with Michael Horovitz. It appears in Weiland's poetry at the time. Several years later, in Taipei, he would try to organize an exhibition of Filliou's work at the Lungmen Gallery. Soon after the visit in Düsseldorf, Mike Dobbie introduced poems by Weiland to readers in Britain in his journal, Street Word. The Ezra Pound expert Massimo Bacigalupo (b. 1947) published excerpts of Weiland's Kallikomi poems in the Rome-based journal Bianco e Nero and used these poems for the soundtrack of one of his experimental films that was screened at the 1970 London Underground Film Festival and later, at the Centre Pompidou. Bacigalupo also mentioned him as a young, promising poet in a book entitled *Notizie di Bamian* that appeared in print in 1970.

In 1973, poems by Weiland that were not written in English but now, in German, were selected by the young poet Jürgen Theobaldy (b.1944) for his journal Benzin. Theobaldy also chose poems by Weiland for the anthology Und ich bewege mich doch (And yet, I move). As the subtitle of the anthology noted, it featured poems from shortly before and shortly after 1968, the year of protests in Paris, Mexico City, Tokyo, Belgrade, Prague, and West Berlin. Many poems at the time breathed an independent spirit of defiance, a typical trait of the anti-authoritarian rebellion of '68 that was loathed by the Right, the "moderate centrists" and the rigidly dogmatic part of the Left, for instance, by the PCF in France.

With Jean-Marie Straub and Danièle Huillet, Weiland corresponded since 1969 when he first

met them and published a text about their Bach-
film in Touch. He also sent them poems he wrote.
In 1975, Jean-Marie Straub translated Weiland's
poem about the film Moses and Aron to French.
Straub got it published in the noted French film
journal Cahiers du Cinéma (Paris), declaring at the
time in this journal, « Il comble à peu tous mes
espoirs quant au film ». Straub added, in a letter to
Weiland, "das Gedicht für uns m'á ému jusqu'aux
larmes, und ich hatte seit dem Tode des Holger M.
nicht mehr geweint! Außerdem, wie Danièle sagte:

Lieber, lieber Andreas,

das Gedicht für uns m'a ému jusqu'aux larmes, und ich hatte seit dem Tode des Holger M. nicht (mehr) geweint! Außerdem, wie Danièle sagte: alles was du uns schreibst, ist endlich eine Antwort auf die Frage, die schon seit Machorka-Muff 1962! — uns beschäftigte: wie kommen solche Arbeiten an bei Menschen guten Willens, die diese Arbeiten in ihrer Klassenexistenz nicht bedrohen? Wir sind nun sehr beruhigt — merci, merci für all diese deine Mühe *

J.-M. Straub, Letter to Weiland, May 11, 1975

Alles was du uns schreibst, ist endlich eine
Antwort auf die Frage, die schon seit Machorka
Muff – 1962 – uns beschäftigte: wie kommen
solche Arbeiten an bei Menschen guten Willens,
die diese Arbeiten in ihrer Klassen-existenz nicht
bedrohen?" ("the poem for us has moved me to
tears, and I had not shed tears (anymore) since the
death of Holger M.! Furthermore, as Danièle said,
it is finally the answer to the question that moved
us since Machorka Muff - 1962! - : how are such
works received by people of good will who are not
threatened by them in their class existence?")

Also in 1975, Weiland met Tony Morgan, the
video artist and live performer. It was Weiland
who wrote the text of Tony Morgan's small
catalogue distributed at the De Appel Gallery in
Amsterdam in early 1976. Both of them went to
Amsterdam for the very first screening in Europe
of Morgan's video film Herman Dances Alone and
a live performance of Morgan at the gallery. At the
time, Morgan dedicated a small painting to Weiland that was later published in Art in Society, an
online art magazine.

In 1976, Weiland went to Taiwan for several years.
Here, he met the writer and filmmaker Yushan
Huang, the writer, choreographer, and dancer Lin
Hwai-min, the poet, painter and song writer Li

Shuangze (b. 1949-d.1977), the composer Ma Shui-long, the young composer Wang Li-de, several artists, the film journalists Ivan Wang and Lee Dawming, and such pro-democracy activists as Wang Jin-ping(1946-2019) and Liang Jingfeng (b.1944). He translated poems by Bai Qiu (= Pai Ch'iu, b. 1936), edited his own journal, and could published in several journals dedicated to the arts, film and literature, among them in Yinxiang (magazine). Prof. Huang Meishu later noted Weiland's relevant assessment of a play by the Taiwanese playwright Yao Yiwei (b. 1922-1997), when he discussed Yao Yiwei's work in the Tamkang Review.

Weiland met the magnificent Vienna-born poet Erich Fried (1921-1988) repeatedly. During a visit in London in the summer of 1981, he gave Fried the manuscript of his Gedichte aus einem dunklen Land (Poems from A Dark Country). On Sept. 10, 1981, Fried wrote the following words about this volume of poems that found no publisher in Germany: "Ich habe schon seit langer Zeit nicht mehr Gedichte gesehen (unveroeffentlichte oder neuerdings veroeffentlichte), die ich fuer so gut und so wichtig halte. Ich meine wichtig, weil sie unsere nicht nur literarische Landschaft bereichern. Dichten ist nicht so sehr eine literarische wie eine menschliche Betaetigung. ... Die Gedichte sind so, dass sie unbedingt veroeffentlicht gehoeren..." In English: "I haven't seen, in a long time, poems (unpublished or recently published ones) that I think are this good and this important. I mean important because they enrich our not only literary landscape. Poetry is not so much a literary activity as a human activity. ... The poems are such that they absolutely deserve to be published."

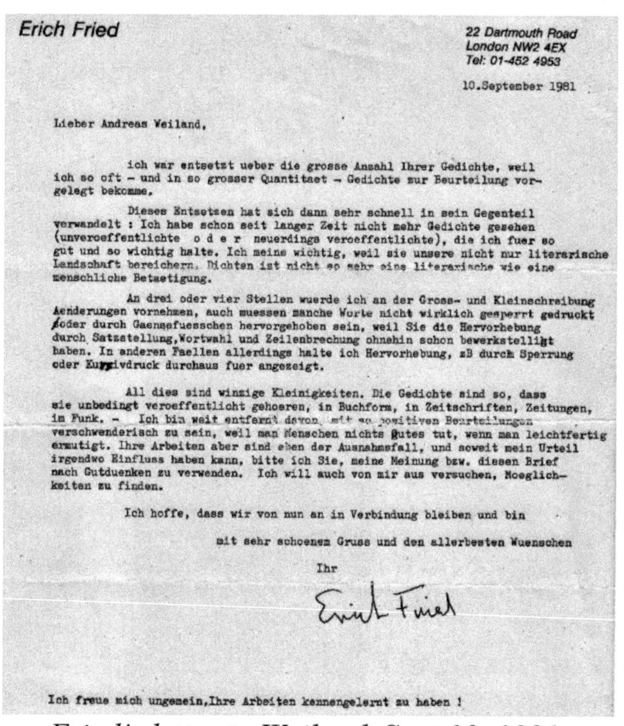

Erich Fried

22 Dartmouth Road
London NW2 4EX
Tel: 01-452 4953

10.September 1981

Lieber Andreas Weiland,

ich war entsetzt ueber die grosse Anzahl Ihrer Gedichte, weil ich so oft — und in so grosser Quantitaet — Gedichte zur Beurteilung vorgelegt bekomme.

Dieses Entsetzen hat sich dann sehr schnell in sein Gegenteil verwandelt : Ich habe schon seit langer Zeit nicht mehr Gedichte gesehen (unveroeffentlichte o d e r neuerdings veroeffentlichte), die ich fuer so gut und so wichtig halte. Ich meine wichtig, weil sie unsere nicht nur literarische Landschaft bereichern. Dichten ist nicht so sehr eine literarische wie eine menschliche Betaetigung.

An drei oder vier Stellen wuerde ich an der Gross- und Kleinschreibung Aenderungen vornehmen, auch muessen manche Worte nicht wirklich gesperrt gedruckt oder durch Gaensefuesschen hervorgehoben sein, weil Sie die Hervorhebung durch Satzstellung,Wortwahl und Zeilenbrechung ohnehin schon bewerkstelligt haben. In anderen Faellen allerdings halte ich Hervorhebung, zB durch Sperrung oder Kursivdruck durchaus fuer angezeigt.

All dies sind winzige Kleinigkeiten. Die Gedichte sind so, dass sie unbedingt veroeffentlicht gehoeren, in Buchform, in Zeitschriften, Zeitungen, im Funk. — Ich bin weit entfernt davon, mit so positiven Beurteilungen verschwenderisch zu sein, weil man Menschen nichts Gutes tut, wenn man leichtfertig ermutigt. Ihre Arbeiten aber sind eben der Ausnahmsfall, und soweit mein Urteil irgendwo Einfluss haben kann, bitte ich Sie, meine Meinung bzw. diesen Brief nach Gutduenken zu verwenden. Ich will auch von mir aus versuchen, Moeglichkeiten zu finden.

Ich hoffe, dass wir von nun an in Verbindung bleiben und bin

mit sehr schoenem Gruss und den allerbesten Wuenschen

Ihr

Erich Fried

Ich freue mich ungemein,Ihre Arbeiten kennengelernt zu haben !

Fried's letter to Weiland, Sept.10, 1981

The comparatist Weigui Fang (b. 1957), an internationally well-known scholar based at Beijing Normal University, refers to this positive assessment uttered by Erich Fried in the "Nachwort" of the book Den Kranich fragen, quoting it in part. He agrees with this assessment of the significance of Weiland's poems, and has mentioned Weiland again later in the introduction of the book Tensions in World Literature: Between the Local and the Universal (London, New York, Singapore: Palgrave Macmillan, 2018), praising him as a poet whose work reveals a "fascination with Beat poetry as a poetically innovative expression of North American 'counter-culture'." Fang interprets this as "opposition to the reactionary cultural 'climate'" prevailing in Germany during the 1950s and much of the '60s. In this regard, Weiland is comparable to Carl Weissner, as Prof. Fang points out. The fact that Weissner and Weiland published poems written in English as well as in German makes them "hybrid" and "cosmopolitical" poems in Fang's opinion whereas Weiland has always said that the German language is "the only fatherland" he has. At the same time, he views the present-day use of the concept "cosmopolitanism" critically, and has often said that he considered himself an internationalist, while giving the term its old meaning of border-crossing solidarity between human beings.

On Jan. 16, 1982, Jean-Marie Straub, who had also received the manuscript of the by then as yet unpublished poetry collection Gedichte in einem dunklen Land, thanked Weiland for "the good poems."

Jean-Marie Straub's card to Weiland.

In 1981 or 1982, the poet Erich Fried offered the manuscript of In einem dunklen Land to Claassen Verlag in Düsseldorf; Jürgen Theobaldy offered it to Rotbuch Verlag in Berlin; Weiland offered part of it to Johano Strasser (Literaturmagazin). The title of the book, later published in Rotterdam (Holland), of course does not only refer to cloudy skies over Germany; it is the lingering Nazi past that appears as so dark.

For German critics, Weiland's poems were too radical. Gabriele Dietze, a professor today and then, the reader at Rotbuch Verlag, wrote in a letter to the poet, dated June 4, 1982, that she preferred Weiland's later poems because those that reflected "the direct political conflicts of the early 1970s" appeared to her "to have become a bit historical", that is, dated. (In German: "Meine Präferenz liegt eher in den zeitlich späteren Gedichten, da die direkte politische Auseinandersetzung der früheren 70iger [sic] Jahre heute schon ein wenig historisch geworden zu sein scheint.") She admitted that the poems could form a good book, but it was *not her "taste."*

Fried, whose independent, absolutely non-conformist stance is well-known, was already meanly attacked by Günter Grass (a member of the Nazi SS as a young man) in the context of Group 47 meetings. It is not by chance that Fried is described as a man "falling between two stools" in Germany in an article published by a Viennese website that commemorates this poet's 100th birthday (https://soal.at/zwischen-den-stuehlen-zum-100-geburtstag-von-erich-fried-1921-1988/). In Germany, Weiland often fell between two stools, too. But as Prof. Weigui Fang mentioned in the "Nachwort" of Den Kranich fragen, an admirable poet like Nicolas Born (1937-1979) called Weiland a "a naturally gifted lyrical poet" (ein geborener Lyriker) in the 1970s, as Jürgen Theobaldy confirms.

With the poet and urbanist Peter Marcuse (1928-2022), a professor at Columbia University in NYC, Weiland was in touch since the mid-1980s when they met. Thus, it was not by chance that Weiland sent his poems to Peter Marcuse. On Nov 18, 1993, Peter Marcuse said about the Poems from A Dark Country that they were written "in the Brecht tradition – clear, sharp, didactic, with nothing excess," adding that the 1975 "Cahier poem seems to me abstractly argumentative; perhaps it just seems discordantly optimistic with hindsight."

Columbia University

IN THE CITY OF NEW YORK

THE GRADUATE SCHOOL OF ARCHITECTURE PLANNING AND PRESERVATION

AVERY HALL

November 18, 1993

Andreas Weiland
Ottostraße 17
52070 Aachen,
Germany

Dear Andreas,

I do appreciate your sending me the poems. I understand very well the compulsion to write poetry; having just come out of the hospital after what could have been major surgery, I put my hand to it too; major crises or sharp insights seem to require a different form of expression.

You write, not unworthily, in the Brecht tradition--clear, sharp, didactic, with nothing excess. The earlier Cahiers poem seems to me to abstractly argumentative; perhaps it just seems discordantly optimistic with hindsight. The 1980's poems are more tangible, solider, it seems to me, becuase they draw their conclusions, and their impact, from events, places, acts.

Marcuse's letter to Weiland, Nov. 18, 1993

In contrast, Marcuse thought that the Poems from A Dark Country were "more tangible, solider, it seems to me, because they draw their conclusions, and their impact, from events, places, acts."

Such praise was rare, but occurred again and again. Thus, a respected poet known for his independent way of thinking and of saying things in East Germany, the poet Volker Braun (b. 1939), wrote Weiland (in an email dated Nov. 20, 2010) about a recently published volume of poems, "Haben Sie Dank für die Zusendung der Gedichte. Ich habe sie gern gelesen, und der Mann, die Haltung, die Orte gefallen mir: Oaxaca, z.B." ("Thank you for sending me the poems. I enjoyed reading them and like the man, the attitude, the places: Oaxaca, for

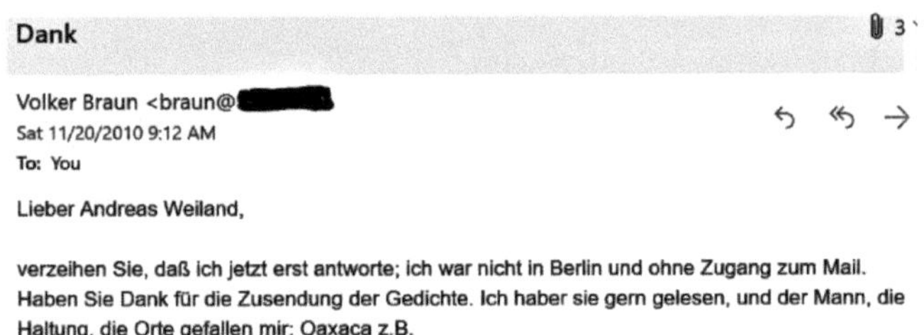

Dank

Volker Braun <braun@

Sat 11/20/2010 9:12 AM

To: You

Lieber Andreas Weiland,

verzeihen Sie, daß ich jetzt erst antworte; ich war nicht in Berlin und ohne Zugang zum Mail. Haben Sie Dank für die Zusendung der Gedichte. Ich haber sie gern gelesen, und der Mann, die Haltung, die Orte gefallen mir: Oaxaca z.B.

example.") Volker Braun's words referred to the author of the poems assembled in the small poetry book entitled höhle, haus, pfad / himmel berg fluß wald and to the fact that one of Weiland's poems in this volume spoke of Oaxaca, another one of Ciudad México. The book's title and subject matter had been suggested by the artist Li

Portenlänger (b.1952); it related to one of her art projects. The book was typeset by Siegfried Höllrigl (Offizin S., Meran) and printed as a bibliophile edition.

Artists like the painter, lithographer, photographer and multimedia artist Luc Piron (b. 1952) and the experimental Belgian filmmaker Karin Mels created films that featured Weiland reading his poetry. Art catalogues published Weiland's poems on various occasions. Several of his poems appeared, for instance, in the catalogue Dekonstruktionen; Vom Widersprechen in Bildern (Deconstructions: Talking Back by Way of Images) dedicated to a solo exhibition of Doris Schoettler-Boll and published by the Rhineland Museum in Bonn. A catalogue edited by the architect Werner Ruhnau (1922-2015) that was published on the occasion of the architectural renewal of the Grillo Theater in Essen and the catalogue Wo bleibst Du, Revolution? (Where Are You Lingering, Revolution?), a catalogue published by Museum Bochum on the 200th anniversary of the French Revolution, also featured Weiland's poetry. Other artists (e.g. Axel Guhlmann, Li Portenbänger, Luc Piron and Angelo Evelyn) included his poems in their artist books, and the filmmaker Werner Nekes added a long poem of Weiland to his book on the film Ulliisses.

Apart from several collections of his poetry, most of them published in Rotterdam (NL), Weiland's poems appeared in a number of books, such as Massimo Bacigalupo's Critica del Novecento / Criticizing the 20th Century, in anthologies, thus in Aiqing de gushi: 350 deutsche Liebesgedichte, published in Beijing, and in the already mentioned anthology Und ich bewege mich doch. Gedichte vor und nach 1968, and then, of course, in various journals, among them the renowned Slovakian literary journal Romboid (No. 8, 2008), published with an introduction by the noted critic Pavel Branko (1921-2020).

I have the joy and honor to transmit the above information about one of our most inspiring and committed poets today to a potentially worldwide readership, and this for the sake of a really rational and humane stance towards life that the œuvre of Andreas Weiland embodies in my opinion.

- Magdi Youssef
  President, Association Internationale d'Études Interculturelles. International Association of Intercultural Studies (I.A.I.S.)

ABOUT THIS BOOK

The poems in this small book created in memory
of Nan Hoover were inspired by works of
Reinhold Bräuer, Ernst Hesse, Nan Hoover,
Mechthild Schienhorst and Martin Schilken that
were chosen for the Düsseldorf exhibition "Um
abermals zu enden: Hommage an Samuel Beckett"
(Kunsthalle Düsseldorf).

When I sent these poems to Michael Erdmann, the
curator of the show, asking him to forward them to
Nan Hoover who had invited me previously to her
apartment in Düsseldorf and shown me how she
created video films like *Returning to Mt. Fuji* with
minimal means, she sent a Thank you note by fax,
saying that these were the first poems ever
dedicated to her.

- Andreas Weiland

PHOTO CREDITS

The **photo** of Nan Hoover was taken in Glasgow
by Myriam Thyes in 2007. The original photo is in
color: The photo is licensed as follows: CC BY-SA
3.0
Source: Wikipedia. File:Nan-Hoover-Glasgow-
2007.jpg
Created: 14 April 2007

The other images used are from the private archive
of Andreas Weiland.

CONTENTS

Stonybrook Editions is an imprint of NHV- Neuer
Horizont Verlag; Steinbeck nr. Bielefeld

Email: new.horizon.press@gmail.com